HERBAL

REMEDIES

FOR

THYROID

DR. RUTH DANIEL

COPYRIGHT

TABLE OF CONTENTS

THYROID DISORDERS

The thyroid is a small butterfly shaped gland located in your neck. Though it weighs only about an ounce, the thyroid gland has some very important functions to carry out that have a major impact on one's health. It maintains body temperature, controls the rate of energy production (including oxygen use and basal metabolic rate), regulates the skeletal and muscular growth of children and heavily influences brain chemistry and thus brain function.

To be able to prevent a disease from happening, it is important to first understand it. And the most important thing to know and understand is the root cause of a disease. What caused this disease in the first place? What experiences or situations did the person do that ultimately led to this disease infecting that person? Once this is understood, it will be easier to prevent that disease from doing any harm to the person.

In the case of thyroid diseases, it's more important to know the root cause of these diseases because the symptoms that they show are usually associated with different diseases or conditions. Now the causes for thyroid problems vary per disease. Some are caused by other thyroid diseases, some are caused by treatment or medication, some are because of a deficiency or an excess of certain nutrients in the body and there are others that are hereditary.

Take Hashimoto's Disease or Hashimoto's Thyroiditis. This is an autoimmune disease wherein your immune system attacks the thyroid gland. The root cause of this disease is unknown, but doctors and scientists identify several factors that may have caused this disease. The two most common causes for this disease is believed to be a genetic flaw and gender. It is believed that genes play a role in a person developing Hashimoto's Disease, though scientists have yet to identify what gene or genes are prone to this disease.

Gender make-up is also believed to play a role as women are more susceptible to develop this disease than men (pregnancy is also believed to be a major factor for developing this disease). Other causes are believed to be iodine deficiency and radiation exposure.

Just like Hashimoto's Disease, the underlying cause of Graves' Disease is also unknown. It is believed that genes and gender play a major role in causing Graves' Disease. Women also have greater risk in developing this disease than men, especially pregnant women. Other factors believed to cause Graves' Disease are stress and infection. Stress and infection might trigger the onset of the disease to people who are prone to getting them but there are no studies that directly link them to the cause of the disease.

It is important to take note of these two diseases as they are the two common causes of most, if not all, of thyroid problems.

One thyroid problem that can be attributed to these two diseases is Thyroiditis. Thyroiditis is the inflammation of the thyroid gland. The most common cause for inflammation in the thyroid is autoimmune disease. In this disease, the immune system malfunctions, causing the antibodies to attack the thyroid gland. Virus and bacteria can also cause Thyroiditis as certain bacteria and viruses attack the thyroid gland directly. Certain drugs such as interferon and amiodarone also cause Thyroiditis because they have the tendency to damage thyroid cells.

Like thyroiditis, Hypothyroidism is also caused by autoimmune disease, particularly Hashimoto's Disease. The damage that the disease causes to the thyroid gland affects the ability of the gland to produce hormones. Autoimmune disease is just one of the causes for Hypothyroidism, there are other factors that cause this conditions and these are:

Treatment for Hyperthyroidism -
Having an overactive thyroid is usually
treated with radioactive iodine or anti-
thyroid medications. There are cases
however where the treatment for
hyperthyroidism caused permanent
hypothyroidism.

Radiation Treatment - Treating cancer
with radiation in the neck and head can
sometimes affect your thyroid and
cause hypothyroidism

Thyroid Surgery - Removing parts or all of your thyroid gland will affect hormone production. It will usually require you to take thyroid hormone medications.

Medications - Certain drugs can cause hypothyroidism like lithium. It is important to consult with your doctor on the effects of the medications you take.

Other possible causes of hypothyroidism are -- congenital

disease, pituitary disorder, pregnancy and iodine deficiency

Another condition that is commonly caused by autoimmune disease, particularly Graves' Disease is Hyperthyroidism. Antibodies that attach itself to the thyroid gland cause it to produce more hormones. Aside from Graves' Disease, other causes of Hyperthyroidism are:

Toxic Nodular Goitre - A solitary hot nodule found in the thyroid can sometimes cause the thyroid to produce more hormones than usual.

Thyroiditis - Inflammation of the thyroid gland can cause it to produce excess hormones that are normally stored in the gland. Subacute thyroiditis and postpartum thyroiditis are the most common thyroiditis that causes Hyperthyroidism.

Medication - Taking thyroid hormone drugs in excess can also cause Hyperthyroidism. It's important to always consult with your doctor before taking any medication to get the proper dosage

Abnormal secretion of TSH - a problem with the pituitary gland may produce an abnormally high secretion of thyroid stimulating hormone (TSH). This will lead to signalling the thyroid gland to produce more hormones.

Thyroid Nodules is also a thyroid problem that is caused by Hashimoto's Disease but the main culprit for Thyroid Nodules is Iodine deficiency. A severe lack of iodine in your diet can cause thyroid nodules. Iodine is needed to produce the hormone thyroxine. Other causes of Thyroid Nodules are:

Overgrowth of normal Thyroid Tissue - This is also called Thyroid Adenoma. It is unclear why this occurs but the thyroid adenoma can sometimes cause the thyroid to produce hormones outside the pituitary glands regulations thus producing more thyroid hormones than needed.

Thyroid Cyst - These fluid-filled cavities (cyst) result from degenerating thyroid adenomas. They are usually benign but can sometimes contain malignant solid components.

Thyroid Cancer - The chances of nodules being malignant are rare. The risk becomes higher though depending on you and your family's medical history.

Damaged Pituitary Gland - Problems with the pituitary gland can also cause Thyroid Nodules.

Goitre is another thyroid problem that is either caused by Graves Disease or Hashimoto's Disease. The enlargement of the gland can be caused by either too much hormone or lack of it. Other causes of goitre are as follows:

Iodine Deficiency - Lack of iodine in the body is actually the main cause of Goitre. It is very essential in the production of thyroid hormones. Goitre is caused when the thyroid enlarges in an effort to obtain more iodine.

Multinodular Goitre - Solid or fluid-filled lumps called nodules develop in both sides of the thyroid. This results in over enlargement of the gland.

Solitary Thyroid Nodules - A single nodule develops in one side of the thyroid gland. This also causes enlargement.

Thyroid Cancer - This is a less common lump that develops in our thyroid gland. The cancer lump can also result in the formation of Goitre.

Thyroiditis - Inflammation of the thyroid gland can also cause Goitre due to the swelling.

Pregnancy - A hormone produced during the first trimester of pregnancy (human chorionic gonadotropin or HCG) can cause Goitre. The gland mistakes HCG for thyroid stimulating hormone (TSH) and enlarges in response to it.

As you can see, it is still unclear as to the real cause of thyroid problems. All problems have several factors to consider, but the real root cause has yet to be identified (save for iodine deficiency). You may notice that a thyroid problem can lead to several more thyroid problems. It's important to always have a check-up with your doctor, especially if you feel something different or abnormal with your thyroid gland.

Taking care of the problem early will help lessen the problem and will save you money.

Additionally the thyroid gland has major influence in all of these areas:

- Enhances a portion of the nervous system called the sympathetic nervous system.
- Promotes breakdown of blood sugar, mobilises fats, essential for protein synthesis, enhances the liver's synthesis of cholesterol.

- Promotes normal adult nervous system function and mood.
- Promotes normal functioning of the heart.
- Promotes normal muscular growth and function.
- Promotes normal GI motility and tone; increases secretion of digestive juices, particularly that of the gallbladder and the stomach.
- Promotes normal female reproductive ability and lactation.

- Promotes normal hydration and secretory activity of the skin.

The thyroid gland takes iodine, which is found in many foods, and converts it into thyroid hormones thyroxine (T4) and triiodothyronine (T3). It is estimated that Iodine makes up about 0.00004% of total human body weight and iodine is found in highest concentration in the thyroid gland cells. These cells combine iodine and the amino acid tyrosine and hydrogen peroxide (using an enzyme called thyroid peroxidase or TPO) to make the hormones T4 (thyroxin) and T3 (triiodothyronine), which are then released into the bloodstream and transported throughout the body attached to a protein called Thyroid Binding Globulin (TBG).

It is important to understand that T4 is an inactive thyroid hormone and about 93% of the thyroid's production of hormone is T4. Only about 7% of the hormone the thyroid gland produces is active thyroid hormone (T3). The 93%

inactive T4 hormone must be converted to T3 in order for this active hormone to generate all the important effects in the body. 60% of T4 is converted to T3 in the liver and 20% is converted into another inactive thyroid hormone called reverse T3 (rT3). Another 20% of T4 is converted to T3 Sulphate (T3S) and triiodothyroacetic acid (T3AC) and is acted upon by the digestive tract bacteria (assuming your digestive tract is in healthy balance of bacteria) and fully converted to T3. Any remaining T4 hormone that wasn't transformed into

T3 or inactive T3 forms will be converted into T3 by the peripheral tissues (such as in brain cells, kidneys and muscle cells).

Only the active T3 hormone exerts a controlling effect on metabolism and all the other functions it governs or modulates. The thyroid is the master gland of your metabolism and so it has a very important job. People who suffer from thyroid malfunction experience many different kinds of health complications affecting a multitude of systems in their body. Every cell in your body has thyroid hormone receptor sites so that little gland affects the function of every cell in your body!

An estimated 27 million Americans suffer from thyroid dysfunction, half of which go undiagnosed. Women are at an estimated 24 times greater risk of developing thyroid malfunction and this risk increases with age and also for those who have thyroid dysfunction within their family.

When the thyroid gland begins to malfunction many doctors neglect to ask the very important question of why. Adrenal problems, hormonal imbalances, poor blood sugar metabolism, irregular immune function and gut infections are all signals that the thyroid might be depressed.

Many times replacement hormones are used in an effort to wipe out symptoms without understanding what has caused the thyroid to malfunction in the first place. More often than not the relief these drugs provide is short-lived, or never really works, because in order to really address the health of the very important thyroid gland, the systems of the entire body must be taken into account. So even though you are taking medications for thyroid dysfunction you may still have problems with your thyroid (even though your TSH levels are in the normal range). For example you can have problems with how the thyroid hormones are transported or how inactive T4 hormone is converted to active T3 hormone. You may have issues with the end effect the thyroid hormone is intended to have at the cell level.

Here is a List of The Influences of Thyroid Hormones on Physiological and Metabolic Function

- Bone: Deficiency of thyroid hormones lead to a decrease in bone development and an abnormal architecture of the bone that is created. Generally, a functionally low (which means low but not flagged as of yet)

serum calcium is noted in hypothyroidism. Elevated thyroid hormones cause an increased serum calcium, as it pulls calcium from the bone, leading to increased risk of pathological fractures of the spine and weight-bearing joints.

- Gastrointestinal Function: Transit time is affected directly by thyroid hormones as is absorption of nutrients.

- Male Hormones: Hypothyroidism has been linked to diminished libido and impotence. Although this condition is more rare in men, it must be considered in treating these conditions.

- Liver and Gallbladder Function: Low thyroid function causes decreased liver clearance and gallbladder congestion through thickening of the bile, often also associated with an elevation of cholesterol. Unfortunately, also often treated with cholesterol lowering drugs while the thyroid function is the cause of the elevated cholesterol.

- Body Composition: As you may know all too well, low thyroid function causes an inability to lose weight. This is caused by a slowed conversion of glucose and fat into energy, and altering the way Human Growth Hormone (HGH) is metabolised in the body.

- Blood Sugar Regulation: Low thyroid slows the insulin response to glucose following eating carbohydrates or sugar and it also slows glucose uptake into cells and tissues, and slows absorption of glucose from the intestinal tract. In other words, your entire energy production system is slowed. It is quite confounding to your body and brain, in that the glucose is in the blood, but the tissues are not able to absorb it. This really confuses the pituitary gland and adrenal glands, resulting in a "stress physiology," even if life is good.

- Cholesterol: As mentioned earlier, low thyroid increases your cholesterol and triglycerides, so your doctor tells you your diet is poor. You become even more strict in your diet, and the tissue starvation (low glucose, low energy) gets worse, which makes the stress physiology worse, which makes your cholesterol higher, which prompts your doctor to put you on cholesterol medication, which interferes with energy production, which further stresses your physiology...whew! You are frustrated!

- Depression: Low thyroid impairs the production of stimulating neurotransmitters, which are the chemicals that antidepressants work on. Low stimulating neurotransmitters leave you, as one of my professors described, feeling "lower than a snake's belly."

- Female Hormones: Low thyroid changes the way oestrogen is metabolised in the body, shifting toward an oestrogen metabolite that has been proven to increase the risk of breast cancer.

- Stress: Low thyroid slows the elimination of the stress hormone cortisol, which leaves you feeling stressed out, not because of "stress," but because the stress hormone can't be removed efficiently.

- Detoxification: Low thyroid slows an enzyme critical for metabolic biotransformation, or detoxification, the process by which the body binds and removes all environmental chemicals, and normal byproducts of metabolism, including hormones. "Toxicity" further slows your metabolism, and leads to headaches and other toxic symptoms.

- Digestion: Low thyroid reduces the release of Gastrin, which determines the output of hydrochloric acid in the stomach, leading to poor protein digestion, sour stomach, and GERD.

- Thermoregulation: Regulation of body temperature is affected by low thyroid, resulting in hot flashes and night sweats, which is especially prominent in perimenopausal women. This is often blamed on oestrogen dropping, but may be directly caused by low thyroid.

- PMS and Infertility: Low thyroid affects the progesterone receptors, making them less sensitive to progesterone, which feels like low progesterone, although the progesterone levels may be normal. Since the activity of progesterone is diminished, the health of the uterus is insufficient for implantation in the second half of the female cycle, leading to difficulties getting pregnant and PMS. Low thyroid also reduces sex hormone binding proteins,

42

leading to an increase in estrogen activity.

- Anaemia: Low thyroid, as mentioned affects protein metabolism, which then lowers the red blood cell mass, which carries oxygen to tissues for metabolism of energy. Yes, another mechanism for feeling lousy.

- Homocysteine: Low thyroid slows a process called methylation, often evidenced by elevated serum levels of homocysteine. Elevated homocysteine in the blood has been proven as a risk factor for cardiovascular disease, Alzheimer's and other neurodegenerative disorders, and cervical dysplasia.

Due to the effect the thyroid hormones have on so many systems of the body, including metabolism and nervous system function, a minimum of two mechanisms can lead to sleep apnea. Number one is the weight gain that typically occurs about the face and often, an enlarged thyroid gland, which can physically impede airflow through the airway, leading to sleep apnea. In addition the reduction in proper thyroid hormone leads to impairment of the part of the brain stem that is in charge of the cardio-respiratory centres, thus leading to abnormal breathing patterns during sleep. Weakened respiratory muscles due to hypothyroid myopathy can be a third cause for sleep apnea.

HERBS AND THYROID

DISORDERS

Like many things, some people are looking for natural alternatives to thyroid hormone replacement or anti-thyroid treatment. While there are no herbs that have thyroid hormone in them, there have been studies evaluating herbs as alternatives or add-ons to thyroid medication.

For the most part, if you do not have a nutritional deficiency, herbs and supplements will not resolve your thyroid condition—and some may cause serious health problems. However, some herbal supplements may help optimise your thyroid function by interacting with the hormones that are already present in your body.

If you are looking into herbal treatments, keep in mind that the effects they have on one type of thyroid disease are not likely to be the same for all types of thyroid disease.

Prevention

Chamomile, sage, and mountain tea have all been associated with a decrease in benign and malignant thyroid disease, and this effect appears to be the strongest for chamomile tea. In one study published in 2015, consuming between two to six cups of these types of herbal tea per week was associated with a reduced incidence of thyroid disease. The reason for this association is not clear, however.

Green tea, interestingly, has been associated with a lower incidence of thyroid disease for some people, but a higher incidence of thyroid disease in others.

Subclinical Hypothyroidism

Subclinical hypothyroidism is characterised by low thyroid hormones levels without symptoms.

Ashwagandha, also referred to as Withania somnifera and Indian ginseng, is derived from a nightshade plant. It is a traditional medicine used in Ayurveda practice that comes in a capsule and powder form. At an average dose of 600 mg per day, it has been shown to reduce thyroid hormone abnormalities in subclinical hypothyroidism in a few small human studies.

Hyperthyroidism (incl. Graves' Disease)

Hyperthyroidism is excessive thyroid hormone activity. Lycopus europaeus, also known as bugleweed, is an herb that has been shown to help reduce the symptoms of mild hyperthyroidism. It may also reduce the symptoms of Graves' disease, an autoimmune type of hyperthyroidism.

Bugleweed is believed to act against the antibodies that cause Graves' disease, but it is not clear why it may reduce symptoms of hyperthyroidism even if you do not have this particular type. It comes as a liquid and a pill, and while it has been well tolerated in human studies, the ideal dose is not established.

In addition, a combination of Yingliu mixture and methimazole has been used for the treatment of Graves' disease in China. Methimazole is an antithyroid medication, and Yingliu mixture is a preparation of oysters, white mustard seed, and a variety of herbs and plants.

A number of studies that used a Yingliu mixture prepared in a laboratory have been carried out in China. Results consistently showed that clinical symptoms and thyroid tests were better with the combination than with the methimazole alone.

Thyroid Tumours

There are many types of thyroid tumours, and some can be quite aggressive, requiring surgery, chemotherapy, and radiation treatment. Fucoidan, which is isolated from the Fucus vesiculosus seaweed plant, has been shown to help control the growth of thyroid tumour cells in a laboratory setting from 2017. It is not clear whether this will work in preventing thyroid tumour growth in humans.

Goitre

A goitre is an enlarged thyroid gland. It can be a sign of hyperthyroidism, hyperthyroidism, or a thyroid tumour.

Iodine Deficiency

Your body needs iodine, an essential mineral, to produce thyroid hormones. Those who are deficient may be advised to increase iodine through diet or supplementation.

There are several types of iodine supplements, including a preparation described as "reduction of 131I," which is made of dried seaweed and other herbs and plants.

While restoring too-low iodine levels is important to thyroid function, such deficiency is very uncommon in the United States and you must be careful about over-consuming iodine either inadvertently or with the best of intentions.

Excessive levels of iodine can cause thyroid disease. They have also been shown to induce hypothyroidism in some people and hyperthyroidism in others. As such, it is best to approach taking iodine-containing herbs and supplements with caution and under the guidance of a healthcare professional.

Herbs are an amazing way to boost good health. They contain essential vitamins and minerals that are often lacking in our modern diet. And they're all natural, so you don't have to worry about side effects that often accompany lab created chemicals. Of course, you may have sensitivities to particular herbs, so it's important to pay attention to how you feel and react to anything new you add. I suggest working closely with a health care provider to be sure you're getting the best combination for your unique circumstances. It's also crucial that you understand what kind of impact these herbs have on thyroid functioning — after all, you don't want to go overboard in either direction. Even natural over- or under-stimulation of the thyroid gland can be a real problem! So let's take a closer look at how these herbs for thyroid support are used.

1. Ashwagandha

This adaptogenic herb has been used for thousands of years, and is especially popular in Ayurvedic medicine. Extensive research has been conducted on the benefits of ashwagandha, and in addition to supporting thyroid health, it's been shown to possess many other beneficial properties. Along with a long history of research indicating a connection between ashwagandha and a positive impact on thyroid functioning, a study published in March 2018 concluded that treatment with ashwagandha may be beneficial to improving thyroid levels in patients with subclinical hypothyroidism.

2. Bacopa Monnieri

Another commonly used herb in Ayurvedic medicine, bacopa monnieri has been found to have positive effects on both hypo and hyperthyroidism. Use seems most effective when taken in conjunction with ashwagandha, green tea, dietary fatty acids, and milk. Research on mice indicated that bacopa monnieri increased levels of T4, indicating it might be an effective treatment for hypothyroidism. It could also be an effective treatment for goitre (enlarged thyroid gland) which occurs when too much TSH collects in the gland, since bacopa monnieri increases T4, which may in turn reduce production of TSH.

3. Black Walnut

Black Walnut is used by many herbalists to treat both goitre and hypothyroidism. Black walnuts contain essential minerals like iodine and manganese, which play a key role in enhancing thyroid function.

4. Ginger

Although technically a spice, not an herb, ginger has been used in herbal medicine for centuries. Ginger has well documented anti-inflammatory properties, and chronic inflammation can cause thyroid disorders. Ginger contains both magnesium and potassium, as well as manganese and the antioxidant compound gingerol.

5. Holy Basil

Also known as tulsi, this herb was considered sacred by Indian royalty, and showed up often in Hindu mythology. Nowadays, this herb has been shown to be effective in balancing mind, body and spirit. Part of the mint family, holy basil is well known as an adaptogenic herb in natural medicine. Chronically high cortisol, caused by ongoing stress, can create a host of problems, including thyroid dysfunction. Holy basil helps your body adapt better to stress. Ginger is one of the easiest home remedies for thyroid which are also most easily available. They are rich in minerals like magnesium and potassium that help to combat inflammation which is also a primary cause of thyroid disorder.

Ginger is readily used as an essential oil. It can also be mixed with other carrier oils and can be applied to the skin.

6. Lemon Balm

This herb has many traditional uses, including encouraging restful sleep, calming stress and anxiety, and relieving indigestion. Research has also shown that it can be beneficial to people with hyperthyroidism. One study showed that the extract prevents the components that over-activate the thyroid from binding with thyroid receptors in patients with Grave's disease. Lemon balm is also frequently used as an antiviral treatment, reducing the load on your liver. Viral infections often go hand in hand with thyroid disorders.

7. Nettle

This is often considered the holy grail of thyroid herbs, because it's effective for both underactive and overactive thyroid issues. Nettle can help turn around iodine deficiency, making it particularly beneficial to those with underactive thyroid. Nettle contains other important vitamins and minerals as well, including Vitamins A and B6, calcium, iron and magnesium. Nettle is also a source of selenium, a trace mineral vital to proper thyroid functioning.

8. Coconut oil

Coconut oil constitutes medium-chain fatty acids that assist in thyroid disease treatment. This oil when consumed in a non-heated form, so benefits from losing weight and increases body metabolism followed by maintaining body temperature too.

Coconut oil is rich in healthy saturated fatty acids, hence when consumed do some thyroid exercise. So, it could work well for thyroid treatment at home.

9. Flax seeds

Flax seeds are well-known home remedies for the thyroid, they are rich in saturated fatty acids and are also good for the heart.

These seeds help in the production of thyroid hormones as they are rich in vitamin b12 and magnesium constituents.

10. Almonds

Nuts are beneficial to our body in some way or the other. Almonds are the best-suited home remedies for thyroid disorders since they are rich in fibre, protein, and minerals.

Almonds contain selenium that is a thyroid beneficial nutrient, they also contain magnesium that makes these nuts beneficial for thyroid cure.

11. Vegetables

Eating vegetables in a natural form improves the functioning of the thyroid gland. So, make a habit to never skip cabbage, spinach, cauliflower, or any other green vegetables. Which benefit and are well-known home remedies for thyroid disorders.

These were the top 10 amazing home remedies for thyroid complications that people can catch up with when facing problems related to thyroid gland functions.

Eating healthy foods and practising regular exercise can help to fight thyroid problems in a better way. Following proper medication along with home remedies manages the thyroid disorder in a short duration of treatment for the same.

Also, there are many supplements available in the market for the sake of thyroid treatment. They are mostly full of iodine, which increases the production of thyroid hormone. But you do not depend on these supplements without talking to a doctor first. Consuming iodine more than the amount can even reduce the production of thyroid hormone.

These supplements are not monitored by any agency and are not quality controlled, hence are usually not suggested by doctors for treatment purposes.

12. Eleuthero

Like Ashwagandha, eleuthero, or Siberian ginseng, is also an adaptogen. Traditionally, it was used to reduce symptoms of fatigue and increase mental alertness and stamina. Adaptogens are thought to work by regulating the hypothalamic-pituitary-adrenal (HPA) axis, which controls the body's response to stress. A dysregulated HPA axis can cause fatigue, sleep disturbances, and may contribute to thyroid disease.

13. Magnolia Bark

Lack of sleep is one big factor for your body's inability to cope with stress. In fact, poor sleep is linked to

obesity, fatigue, and other conditions driven by hormonal imbalances. at the same time, an underactive thyroid may make it harder to get the sleep you need.

Magnolia bark effectively promotes better sleep via its power to increase GABA, a calming neurotransmitter. People with reduced GABA are prone to insomnia or other sleep problems. Magnolia bark also has a long history in traditional Chinese medicine as an anxiety and stress soother, which makes it great to help you get restful sleep.

14. Bacopa

Bacopa is mostly known for its beneficial effect upon mood and mental clarity, but an animal study demonstrated that bacopa increased thyroid hormone production as well. High-dose bacopa extracts increased both T3 and T4 similar to that of the levothyroxine, stimulating the thyroid gland and alleviating symptoms .

15. Black Cumin Seed Oil

Black cumin may have significant beneficial effects on patients with

Hashimoto's thyroiditis. Black cumin seed oil also has anti-fungal, anti-inflammatory, and cholesterol-reducing properties.

After 8 weeks of treatment, participants receiving black seed oil experience reduced BMI, a reduction in inflammatory markers, and a significant decrease in anti-TPO antibodies. They also experienced an increase in both T4 and T3 thyroid hormone levels. Reducing thyroid antibodies may also help improve symptoms of anxiety. A 2004 study found a link between anxiety or mood disorder and the presence of TPO antibodies.

16. Coleus

Various environmental toxins and heavy metals can damage the thyroid, hindering the production of thyroid hormone and causing fatigue, brain fog, and other symptoms.

In animal studies, an herbal blend containing coleus, along with bacopa and ashwagandha, restored thyroid function after exposure to harmful environmental chemical compounds. There are many environmental compounds that can deplete both T4 and T3 thyroid hormones, and this blend was successful in restoring healthy thyroid function in subjects whose thyroid had been damaged by toxins.

Other herbs for thyroid hormones

Sea kelp (Ascophyllum nodosum) and bladderwrack (Fucus vesiculosus) are dietary sources of natural iodine, which is essential for thyroid function, but you should practice caution with these herbs. In excess, iodine can further harm the thyroid for those with autoimmune disease like Hashimoto's. If you suspect an iodine deficiency, natural sources can help address this deficiency, but it's important to talk with your holistic doctor if you're unsure.

Quick Tips to Make These Herbs Part of Your Daily Routine

So now you know which important herbs for thyroid support are, but how do you get enough of them to make a difference? Again, I suggest working with a professional to determine which herbs are best for your specific situation — remember, some work on hypothyroidism, others on hyperthyroidism, and you don't want to inadvertently make your situation worse!

Brew some tea. Drinking tea is a great way to relax and decompress when you need a quiet moment. Why not add a little extra oomph to your ritual by choosing thyroid supporting herbs to make your soothing brew?

Take a high-quality supplement. Let's face it, it's sometimes hard to find ways to get all of these great herbs in regularly. One of the easiest ways to make sure you are getting a medicinal dose is by taking supplements designed for a specific purpose – like supporting your thyroid.

Throw them in smoothies. If you're used to drinking your breakfast, just add a bit of flavour and texture with some of the above herbs. Lemon balm is a particularly nice addition, adding just a hint of lemon.

Find a new recipe – or add some of these herbs to your standard meal rotation for a new twist! Food can be amazingly flavorful when you add the right blend of herbs, spices, and extracts. While some of these herbs may not taste great, others can perk up an old recipe or help you find a new favourite.

Keep an eye on stress levels. Stress and thyroid problems go hand-in-hand for many women. While it's not always realistic to eliminate all stress, we want to make sure your body isn't experiencing the adverse effects. Set aside time to commit to yourself each week, don't hesitate to lean on others for help, and, remember—self-care isn't selfish.

Try inositol with selenium. A combination of myoinositol and selenium has been shown to restore healthy thyroid function in patients diagnosed with thyroid autoimmune disorders. Myoinositol and selenium are also beneficial for hyperthyroidism, as with Graves' disease, restoring TSH levels and normal thyroid hormone levels.

Omit gluten, at least temporarily. Gluten can be problematic for thyroid health for many people—myself included. Gluten can worsen autoimmune thyroid issues, causing your immune system to mistakenly flag your thyroid gland for destruction. If you're unsure, try eliminating gluten for 3-6 months and see how you feel.

Dial in your diet. Your thyroid needs an array of nutrients to function properly, like B12, zinc, iodine, other minerals, and amino acids. Prioritise quality proteins like pastured poultry, eggs, and fish, a variety of plant foods like leafy greens, broccoli, zucchini, and other vegetables, and healthy fats from avocado, olive, coconut, and ghee. If you're struggling with hormone health (that includes your thyroid), a vegan or vegetarian diet may not be best at this time.

Are Natural Treatments Effective?

Natural remedies can be effective for improving overall health and for treating subclinical thyroid problems. For people with mild thyroid conditions, going natural may have an advantage over prescription medication in that natural treatments typically have fewer side effects. For people taking thyroid medication, herbal treatments and dietary changes should be approved by a doctor because combining different forms of treatments can create unwanted side effects.

Your thyroid is a powerhouse for your overall health and well-being. When it's not functioning properly, it can be the root of many problems, including unexplained fatigue and weight gain.

While sometimes medication is necessary to restore thyroid function, lifestyle and diet are a crucial piece of overall thyroid health. These herbs are just a few that have been shown to be helpful in protecting your thyroid now so it can keep working for you for many years to come. Which herb is right for you? Talk to your holistic healthcare provider today about how you can best protect your thyroid health.

There you have it, thank you for choosing my book. If you find this book helpful, I would appreciate you letting other readers know about it by leaving a book review. I wish you all the best.

Printed in the USA
CPSIA information can be obtained
at www.ICGtesting.com
LVHW020203031123
762966LV00011B/206

9 798352 181218